level 2

mastering t

"To me, the piano
is like a musical world –
it takes me to a place
beyond reality."

Lang Lang

FABER *ff* MUSIC

"You should now be playing your scales hands together. Try to work on the moments when you change your hand position, when your thumb goes under."

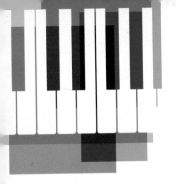

"Before
playing chords
you must check
that you have
a good hand
position.
It's about
being comfortable
and making sure
your wrists are
relaxed and not
stuck."

"For me, phrasing is like having a conversation. Each phrase is a sentence in that conversation – sometimes you include a comma because you have more to add and sometimes you finish the sentence."

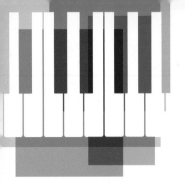

"Both hands need to work together but also be free to do individual things. You will only manage that after lots of practice with separate hands."

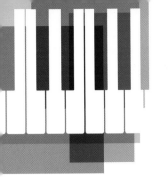

"When I was nine, one of my first piano lessons at the Beijing Conservatory was about learning how to release my energy through my arm. By using my arm weight I learnt to play a really good 'forte'."

"I love to find
inspiration away from
the music when I'm
learning a new piece.
Here are some
paintings and ideas
which help me capture the mood
of some of the pieces in this book."

Contents

Introduction

I've created the *Mastering the piano* series with my partner Faber Music to get today's kids really enthused about playing the piano: to inspire them to perform with love, energy and commitment. This series captures my own passion for piano playing and shares my artistic values and technical insights with the next generation of pianists.

There are no shortcuts to becoming a pianist: good playing can only be achieved through good work. This book sets out to give players the advice, resources and the desire to reach this goal. Over the course of eight units, I explore key aspects of piano technique and offer advice and suggestions on the challenges encountered. Each unit includes exercises, a study and two pieces to learn; I've selected some of the best-loved works from the great European tradition as well as some really extraordinary arrangements of world music that I love.

This book is not a tutor, so you do not need to work through it progressively. Pick and choose what you would like to focus on depending on your own individual needs and tackle the units in an order that suits you.

In addition to the printed books, materials supporting the series are available from langlangpianoacademy.com. This multi-platform delivery of learning provides an engaging format for tech-savvy young learners.

To me, the piano is like a musical world – it takes me to a place beyond reality. You, too, will find that it extends your mind, heart, creativity and communication skills. You don't need a concert hall; you don't need a big grand piano: any piano is enough – and the world will be yours to embrace.

Lang Lang

LANG LANG

INTERNATIONAL
MUSIC FOUNDATION

Exploring the keyboard

Message from Lang Lang

In this unit I would like you to start moving all around the piano keyboard with more confidence. We're going to get used to travelling smoothly and swiftly and playing high up and low down.

Warm up **jumps and crosses**

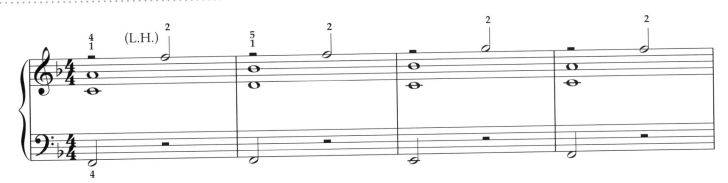

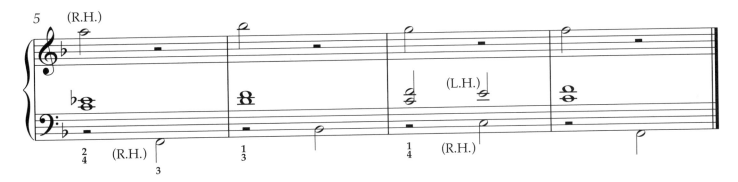

▶ Learn the chords at the start of each measure / bar first: can you play them without looking at your hands?

▶ Next fill in the notes that jump and cross hands. Play them with confidence, always being aware of where your hand is going.

Reminder

Keep a soft, curved hand position and relaxed arms and shoulders even when you are moving quickly around the keyboard. Have fun!

Study in C

Felix Le Couppey
Op.17 No.18

This study will get you moving around the keyboard and crossing your hands over smoothly and confidently. You can use pedal (one per bar) in this study too if you like.

Moderato ♩ = c.116

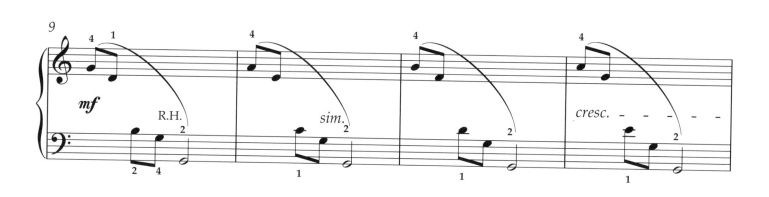

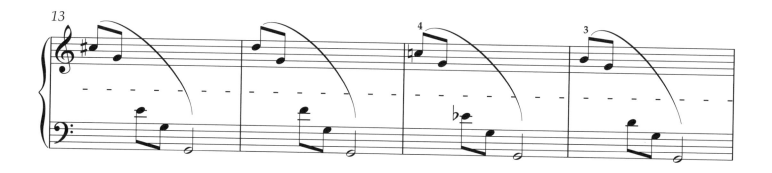

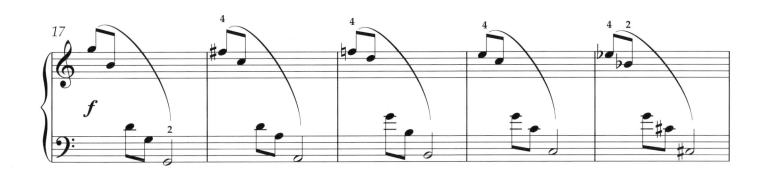

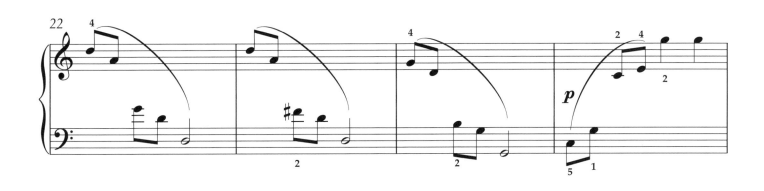

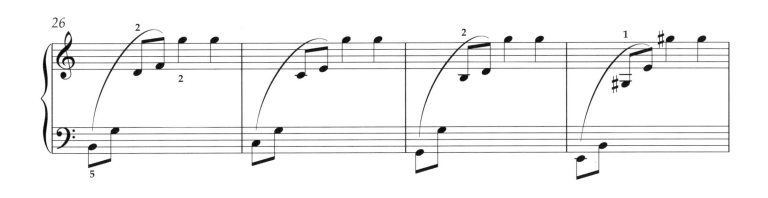

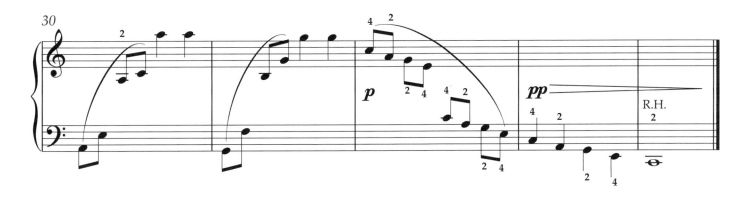

Bear dance
from 'Album for the young' Op.68

Robert Schumann

You can't look at your hands in this unusual piece! Your right hand should be two octaves higher than written, but if you find this is too far just play it one octave higher.

Allegretto pesante ♩ = 72–78

FINE

D.C. al Fine
(senza replica)

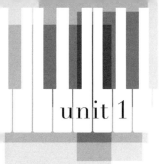

Ecossaise in G

Johann Wilhelm Hässler

In this upbeat piece you need to move your right hand quickly and confidently, bouncing down the keyboard in groups of 3 notes.

Hand coordination

Message from Lang Lang

One of the most important skills for a pianist is good hand coordination: making sure notes sound exactly together when you play. To improve your hand coordination you need to listen carefully to how you play and develop good control.

Warm up **copying and contrasting**

Listen carefully to make sure both hands are perfectly coordinated.

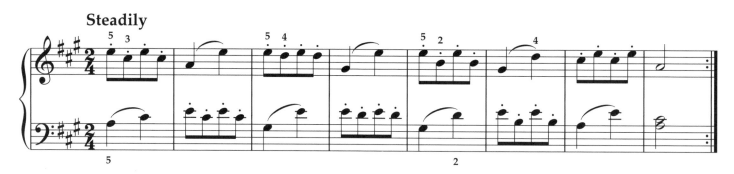

Try these variations to develop independent hands:

▶ Try one hand legato and the other staccato.

▶ Try one hand 'forte' and the other 'piano'.

▶ Try both hands legato but vary the dynamics between the hands.

If you managed these three variations then you are beginning to develop independence between the hands. Allowing one hand to play with a different dynamic or articulation to the other is vital for expressive playing.

Reminder

Remember you must learn each hand separately first!
Try listening more to the hand with the tune as you play.
This helps make it slightly louder than the other hand.

Study

Albert Loeschhorn
Op.65 No.2

Both hands have a lot to do in this study, so really concentrate on exact coordination. Notice that each hand has the tune at different times – make sure the tune sings out.

Melody Arabian Air

Felix Le Couppey

Lots of close work between the hands means careful listening to make sure this piece is well coordinated. Playing the staccato notes exactly together will give it real impact!

To begin with

Nicolai von Wilm
Op.81 No.1

This is great for getting used to a common left-hand accompaniment pattern. Make sure it isn't too loud – the right hand tune must be clearly heard above it!

Rhythmic control

Message from Lang Lang

Playing with a good sense of rhythm is extremely important for all pianists. In this unit we will get used to playing in $\frac{6}{8}$ time and we'll also explore rhythmic control by looking at changes of tempo. It's so important to be able to change the tempo but still feel a clear beat.

Warm up 1 **rollercoaster**

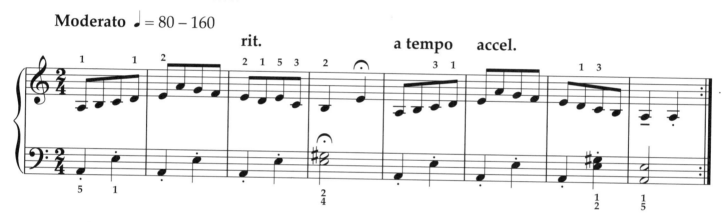

▶ Learn the notes in this exercise first, keeping the same tempo throughout.

▶ Make sure you know what all the terms mean, then play the piece with the changes of tempo.

▶ Keep feeling the beat throughout - even when it speeds up or slows down!

Reminder

The $\frac{6}{8}$ time signature means there are 6 x ♪ beats in each measure/bar.
Each measure/bar can be grouped into 2 beats: ♫♫ ♫♫ = ♩. ♩.

You will need to find out what all these terms means for this unit:

A tempo ....   Molto ....

Accel. (accelerando) ....   Poco ....

Allegramente ....   Rall ....

Giocoso ....   Rit. (ritenuto) ....

Marc. (marcato) ....   𝄐 ....

Study in D

Carl Czerny
Op.187 No.49

unit 3

A simple little study to get you used to the flowing feel of $\frac{6}{8}$.

A joke
from 'For children'

Béla Bartók

Learn this piece at a steady speed before attempting the tempo changes. Then have some fun with it. Why do you think it is called 'A joke'?

Tarantella

Alan Bullard

Here is a great piece to enjoy the feeling of $\frac{6}{8}$ rhythms. Learn it slowly at first but speed it up when you can - it should sound intense and dramatic!

unit 4

Phrasing

Message from Lang Lang

For me, phrasing is like a conversation. Each phrase is a sentence in that conversation. Sometimes you include a comma because you have more to add and sometimes you finish the sentence. You're now at a level where you should start to think about phrasing in all your pieces.

Say this out loud: "I love the piano."

▶ Notice that you don't say each word in the same way. Try saying it four times, emphasizing a different word each time and notice the difference it makes.

▶ It's the same in music - you need to know which notes are the important ones within a phrase. Often the composer helps us by including hairpins to indicate this.

Here is a famous pianistic phrase. It has no words, it speaks for itself:

▶ Play these bars, thinking about how the music should be phrased.

▶ Write in how you phrased it, using dynamics and hairpins.

▶ Try phrasing pieces you are learning in different ways.

Have a go!

Try writing a tune for some words. It could be a short poem, a sentence or just your name. Think about where you would breathe and the meaning of the words. Which note is the most important in the phrase? Add some dynamics.

Study in D minor
from 'The wheel of progress'

Thomas Dunhill
Op. 74 Book 1

The phrasing is clearly marked by the composer in this legato piece. Make sure you include all the details when you play it.

Allegro non troppo ♩ = *c*.92

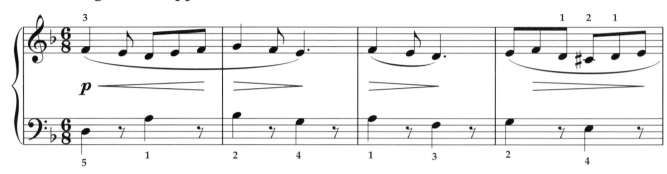

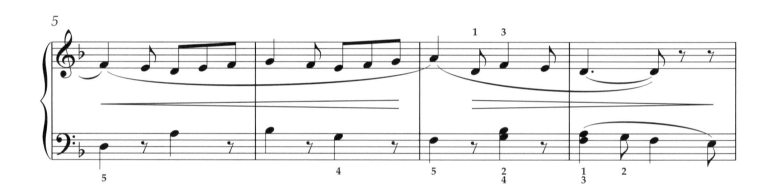

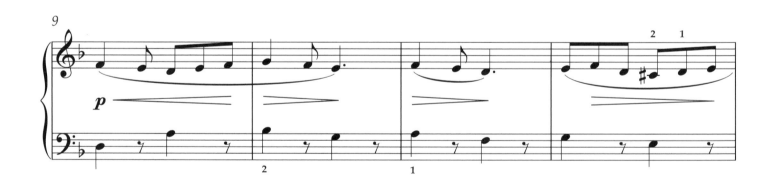

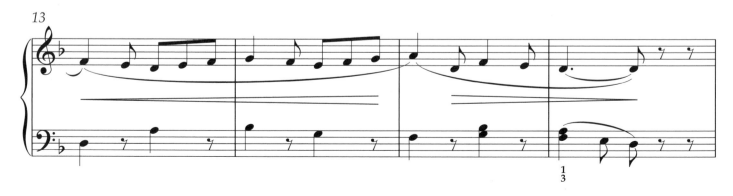

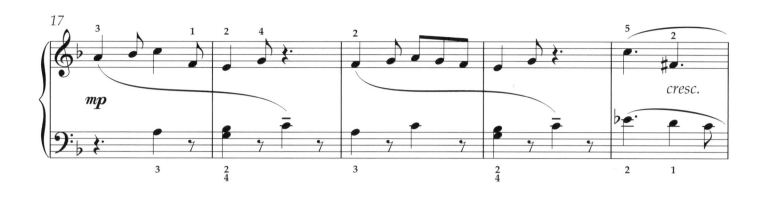

Night journey

Cornelius Gurlitt

This time your left hand is in charge of the phrasing! Make sure the right hand is very quiet and let the left hand really sing out the phrases.

Takeda lullaby

Traditional Japanese
Arranged by Alan Bullard

Imagine this beautiful Japanese lullaby being sung. Consider where the singer would take a breath and show that in your playing. Imagine how the singer's voice would sound.

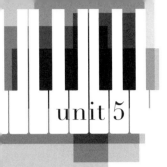

Developing dexterity

Message from Lang Lang

" I think everyone wants to play fast! Let's work on your dexterity by focusing on short groups of fast notes. By working in short bursts you can focus on tricky fingerings (such as putting the thumb under) and gradually speed up your fingers. It's a method I used to improve my own dexterity at the piano when I was young.

Warm up **Arabesque exercise**

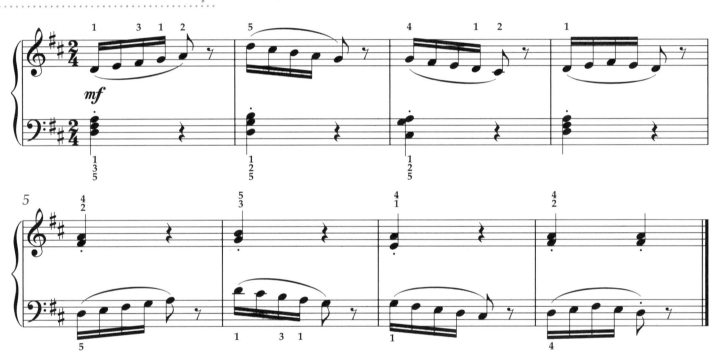

Warm up **Brain teaser**

You should now be playing your scales hands together but do try this warm up hands separately first.

Not too fast

>> For a list of hands-together scales for this level see **langlangpianoacademy.com**

Étude

Felix Le Couppey
Op.17 No.6

This is a great study for rapid fingerwork and will prepare you for *Arabesque*. Make sure all the groups are even and secure. Any that aren't should be taken out and repeated several times.

Arabesque

Johann Friedrich Burgmüller
Op.100 No.2

➤➤ You can hear me perform this for you online.* Remember to show off your great fingerwork and enjoy the sparkling sound as the groups of notes fly up the keyboard.

➤➤ * langlangpianoacademy.com

Gypsy dance

Joseph Haydn

Another piece to dazzle with! This is a right-hand finger twister so it will require plenty of slow, separate hand practice to prepare. Follow the fingering carefully.

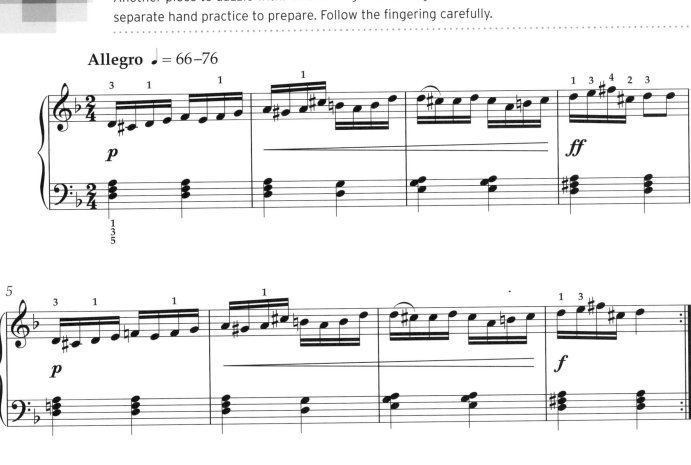

Finger control

Message from Lang Lang

Everyone has a stronger thumb and weaker 4th and 5th fingers. In this unit we're going to begin by working on our weaker fingers. Then we're going to play some strong, 'forte' music to strengthen our playing and add volume.

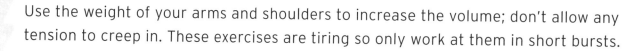 You can work at these away from the keyboard, too. Tap the same patterns out on a table or book: you should be able to hear your fingers drumming the rhythm.

▶ Check all the notes are even and equal in weight.

Reminder

Use the weight of your arms and shoulders to increase the volume; don't allow any tension to creep in. These exercises are tiring so only work at them in short bursts.

Stately study

Alan Bullard

Take your time with this study – it is all about playing with weight and a full tone, which is better if it is not rushed. Use your arm weight and keep your shoulders relaxed.

Trumpet voluntary

Jeremiah Clarke
Arranged by Alan Bullard

Imagine a grand procession as you play this: it should not sound rushed. Aim for a warm, rich tone. Check what speed you can comfortably play the trills – this will decide your tempo.

Soldier's march
from 'Album for the young' Op.68

Robert Schumann

This piece will need lots of practice with separate hands before you put it together. The chords must be short and crisp – the rests are as important in this piece as the chords themselves.

The left hand

Message from Lang Lang

It's time to focus on your left hand now. Apart from having the occasional tune, your left hand spends a lot of time accompanying the right. It's important to work at these accompaniment patterns so you can play them smoothly and quietly, allowing the right hand to sing out above.

Warm up **Left-hand finger twister**

▶ This gentle warm-up will loosen up your fingers.

▶ Concentrate on a good hand position and playing without tension.

Warm up **Left-hand accompaniment pattern**

▶ Keep all the notes even. Make sure the thumb notes aren't any louder than the rest.

▶ Play quietly, imagining the right-hand tune singing out over the top.

Reminder

It's very important to keep your left hand in a relaxed, curved shape when you're playing these accompanying passages.

Study

Stephen Heller

Work hard on your left hand, making sure it's smooth and even before you add the right hand.
Remember the right hand should be slightly louder, so it can sing out over the left.

Cello solo

C.S. Lang

In this beautiful piece your left hand has the starring role – imagine the sound of a cello as you play. Keep the right hand chords very quiet so they don't overpower the left.

40

Song

Carl Reinecke
Op.183 No.1

Your left hand is back to creating a quiet, smooth accompaniment in this piece. Follow the dynamics and phrasing in both hands, but with the right always singing out above the left.

Dynamics

Message from Lang Lang

I would like you to really focus on dynamics in this unit, and also the Italian terms in music that describe how you should play a piece. Remember: you will need to use the weight of your arms to play a really good 'forte'.

Warm up **Dynamic workout**

Reminder

It may help you remember all the dynamics if you mark them in different shades on the page. Make sure you know all the Italian terms, too. Here's a list from this unit:

A tempo back to the original tempo
Allegretto scherzando moderately quick and playful
Dolce sweetly
Molto lentamente, con espressione very slowly, with expression
Molto rit. (ritenuto) slowing down a lot
Più *f* even louder
Poco a poco cresc. (crescendo) gradually getting louder
Poco allarg. (allargando) broadening out a little
Rfz (rinforzando) reinforcing (emphasized)

Study in dynamics

Alan Bullard

unit 8

There are lots of details to work on here: don't miss any of the dynamics and make sure you know what all the Italian terms mean!

Dedication

Stephen Heller

This delicate piece needs subtle variation in dynamic; none of it should be too loud. The notes which are 'forte' should have a warm rather than hard sound.

Molto lentamente, con espressione ♩ = 44

Dance of the sugar plum fairy

Pyotr Ilyich Tchaikovsky
Arranged by Peter Gritton

unit 8

This last piece is a challenge for you! It's a very famous tune
from *The Nutcracker* ballet, set in the Land of Sweets.

from Simply Classics Grades 2-3
© 2007 by Faber Music Ltd

© 2014 by Faber Music Ltd and Lang Lang.
All rights administered by Faber Music Ltd.
This edition first published in 2014
Bloomsbury House 74-77 Great Russell Street
London WC1B 3DA
Music processed by Jeanne Roberts
Cover and page design by Chloë Alexander Design
Photography by Rhys Frampton
Printed in the USA
All rights reserved

Lang Lang: worldwide management - Jean-Jacques Cesbron,
CAMI Music, New York (www.camimusic.com)
Lang Lang: UK/Ireland management - Steve Abott,
Rainbow City Broadcasting Ltd (www.rainbowcity.co)

ISBN10: 0-571-53852-5
EAN13: 978-0-571-53852-2

Lang Lang is an exclusive recording artist with Sony Classical.

His latest album releases include:
Lang Lang: Live in Vienna
Lang Lang: The Chopin Album
Lang Lang/Simon Rattle: Prokofiev 3 Bartók 2
Lang Lang: Liszt My Piano Hero

Well done on completing my Level 2 book!
Look out for the other books in my series:

Early Elementary (Grade 1)
0-571-53851-7

Late Elementary (Grade 3)
0-571-53853-3

Early Intermediate (Grade 4)
0-571-53854-1

Intermediate (Grade 5)
0-571-53855-X

To buy Faber Music publications or to find out about the full range of titles available
please contact your local music retailer or Faber Music sales enquiries:

Faber Music Ltd, Burnt Mill, Elizabeth Way, Harlow CM20 2HX
Tel: +44 (0) 1279 828982 Fax: +44 (0) 1279 828983
sales@fabermusic.com   fabermusicstore.com